kidsPERIENCES with Kayen!

BECOMING A BIG BROTHER

story and images by
Himanshu J. Suthar

edited by Debbie Ogilvie

dedicated to my two loves,
Kayen and Laiya

goldenmoondesign.com © 2017

Once upon a
time there
was a 4-year-
old boy named
Kayen who
went to
preschool
everyday.
   One day, he
was picked up
early by his
mom and dad.

As Kayen's dad buckled
him in his car seat, he said.
"We are taking mommy to
the doctor and have a big
surprise for you."

Kayen wondered why his mommy needed to visit the doctor and what the big surprise for him would be?

After a 20-minute car ride, Kayen saw a big building with big windows. It was the doctor's office.

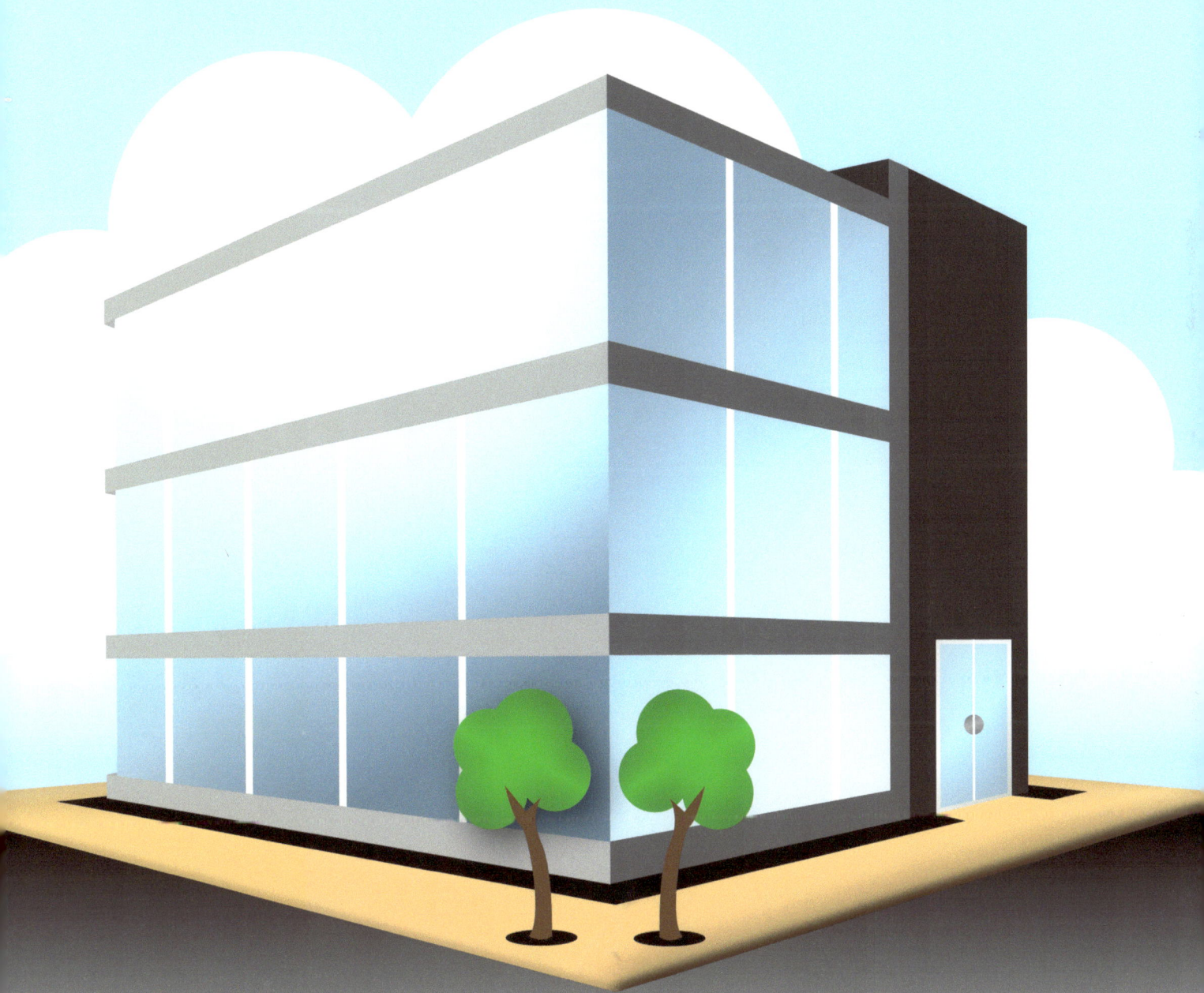

Kayen's dad parked the car and put it right between the orange lines just like the other cars.

They walked into the doctor's office and sat in the waiting area. Lucky for Kayen there were a bunch of fun toys for him to play with.

After 10 minutes, the door opened and the nurse called
for **Kayen's** mom.

The nurse took them to a room that had a computer with a large screen called an ultrasound machine. The doctor told Kayen's mom to lay on the table and show her tummy.

"Does mommy have a tummy ache?" Kayen asked.

"Well, let's find out what's in there," said the doctor.

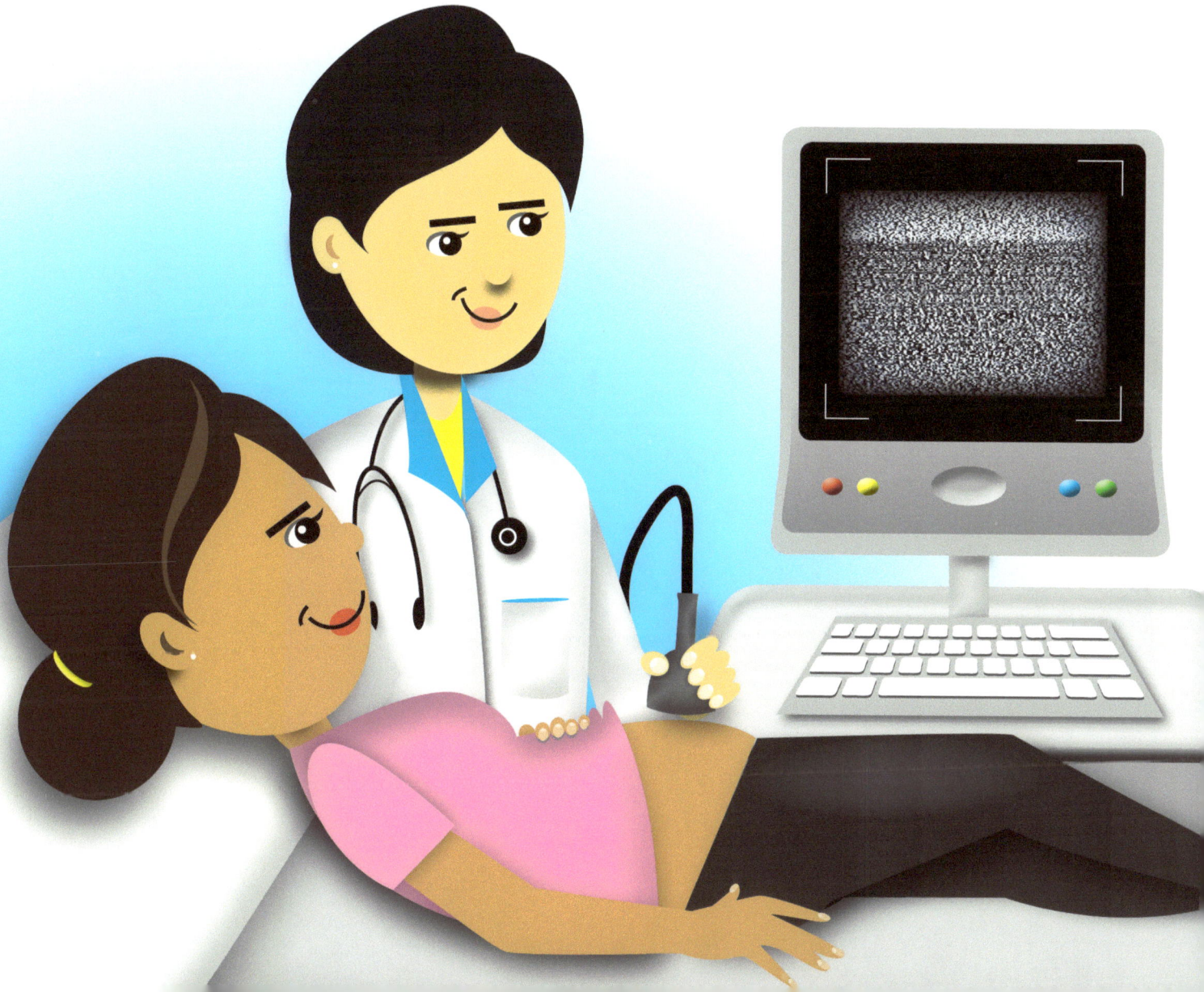

The doctor put a slippery gel on his mom's tummy so that a tool from the ultrasound machine could slide around to look for something in there. For fun, she spelled KAYEN!

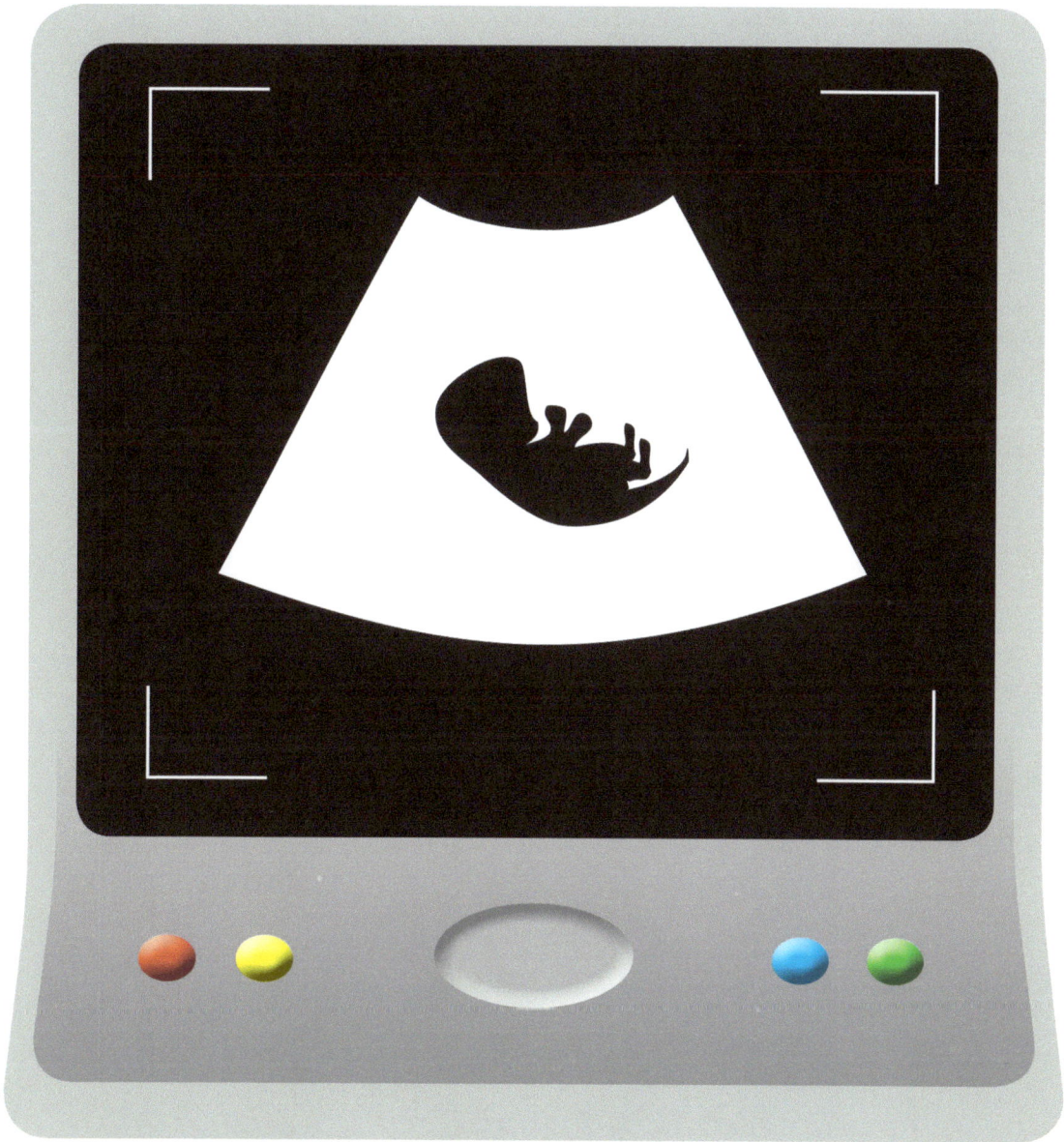

The ultrasound found something and Kayen could see it on the large screen. The doctor said it's tiny and is the size of a bean. "It looks like mommy had shrimp for lunch," Kayen said.

"Surprise, you're going to
be a big brother!"
his mom and dad said at
the same time.

Kayen was confused. "Am I going to be the big brother of a shrimp?" he asked.
    "No silly goose, that's a baby growing in my tummy and it needs about 9 months to grow full-sized," his mom laughed.

What a great surprise! Kayen was super-excited about becoming a big brother and couldn't wait to meet this baby.

Month by month,
Kayen saw his
mom's tummy
grow bigger. This
was because the
baby inside was
growing. His mom
called it her
baby bump.

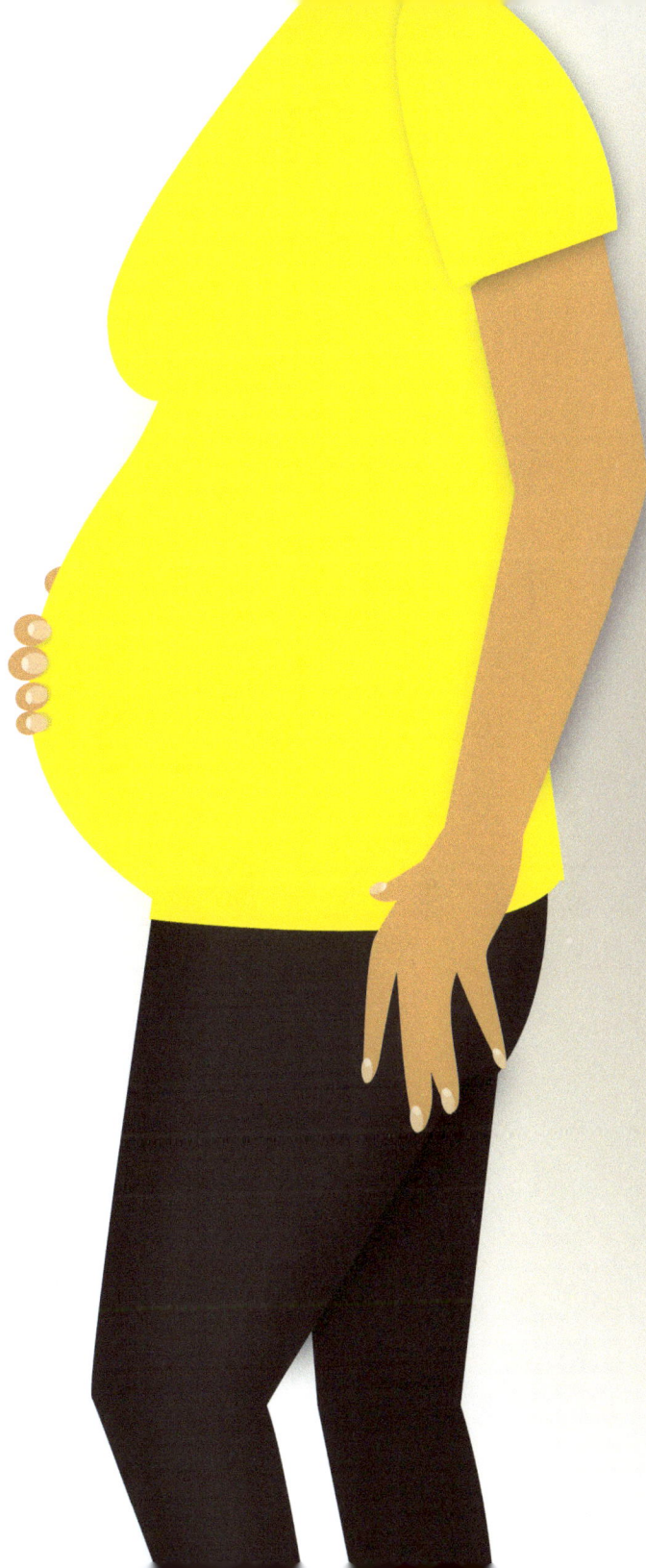

Kayen noticed his mom's feet getting puffy. She said because of all the changes in her body needed for the baby to grow, her feet become puffy which means they are swollen. But not to worry, it was normal.

The next day they went to the doctor and she told Kayen's mom to rest with her feet up so the swelling goes down. Then she used the ultrasound machine on his mom's tummy again.

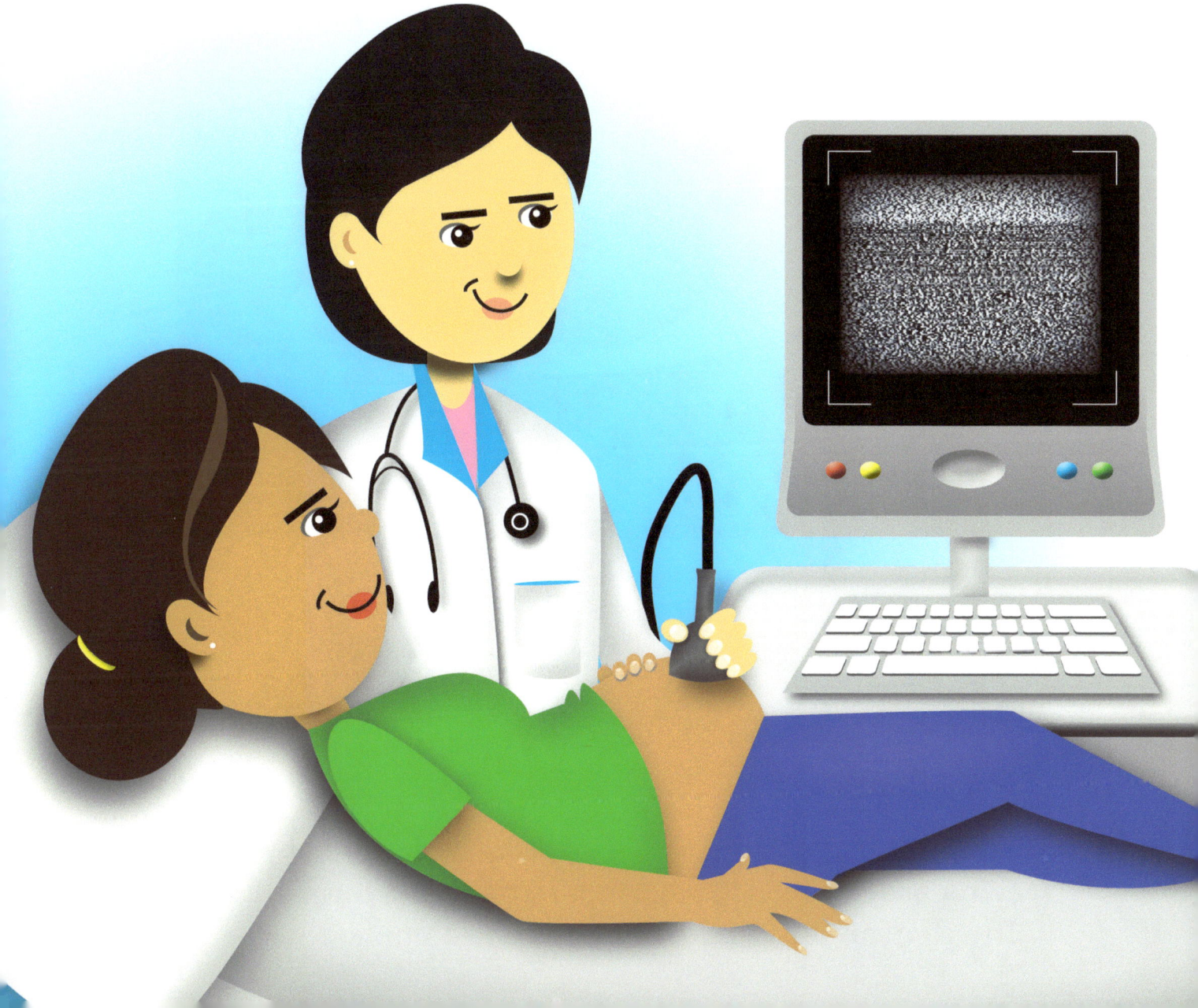

This time, instead of a shrimp, Kayen saw a baby! It was moving around like it was swimming in his mom's tummy. The doctor said the baby was about the size of a lemon.

The doctor took several pictures of the baby with the ultrasound machine and printed them out on paper. Kayen was excited to take them home and share them with his family and friends.

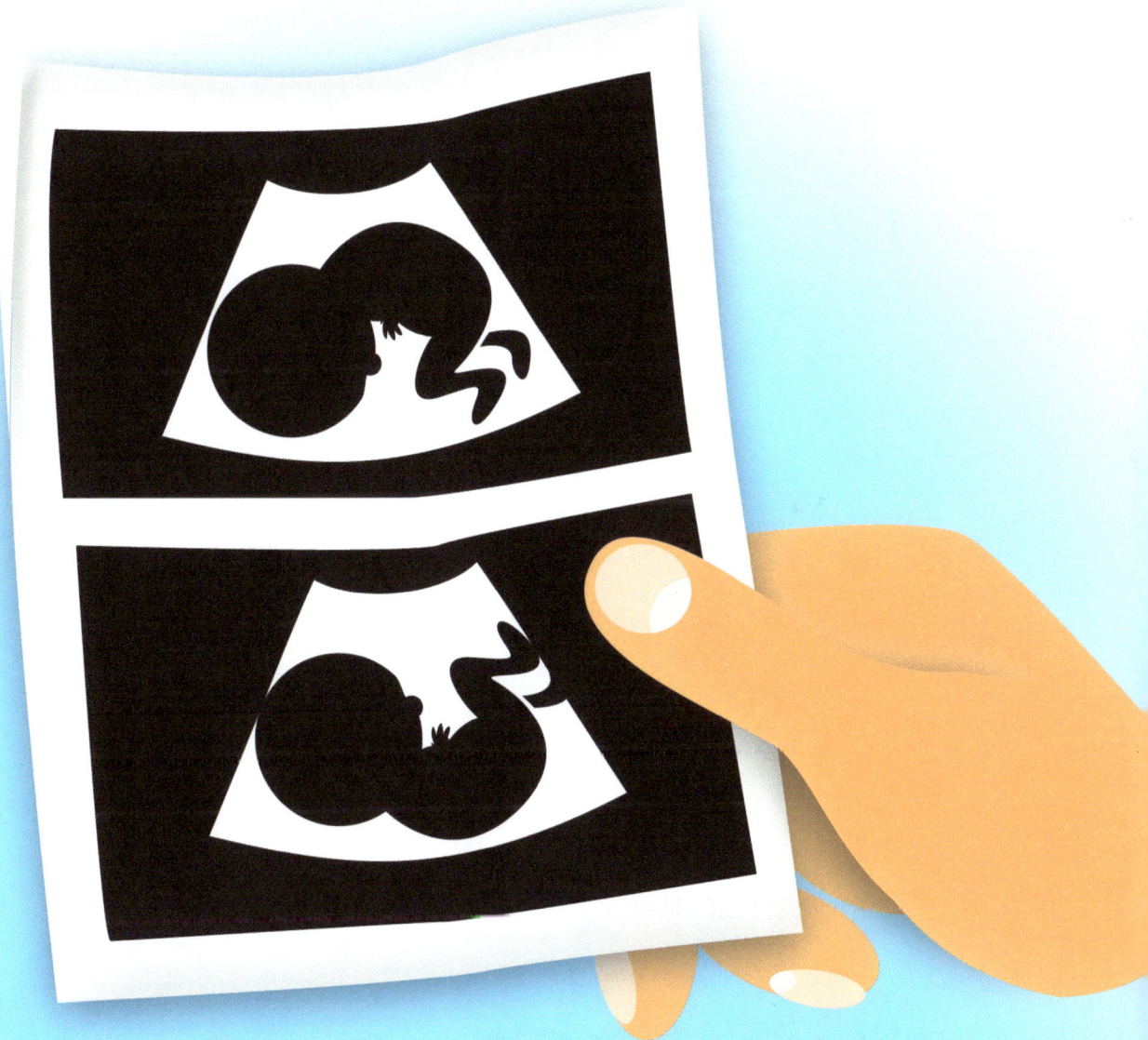

After seeing the ultrasound pictures, Kayen wondered if he would be getting a baby brother or sister. His mom and dad said it would be a surprise until the baby was born.

The baby inside
Kayen's mom's
tummy was still
growing. It looked
as if she had a
basketball in there.
She started feeling
tired and achy
which made it hard
for her to walk.

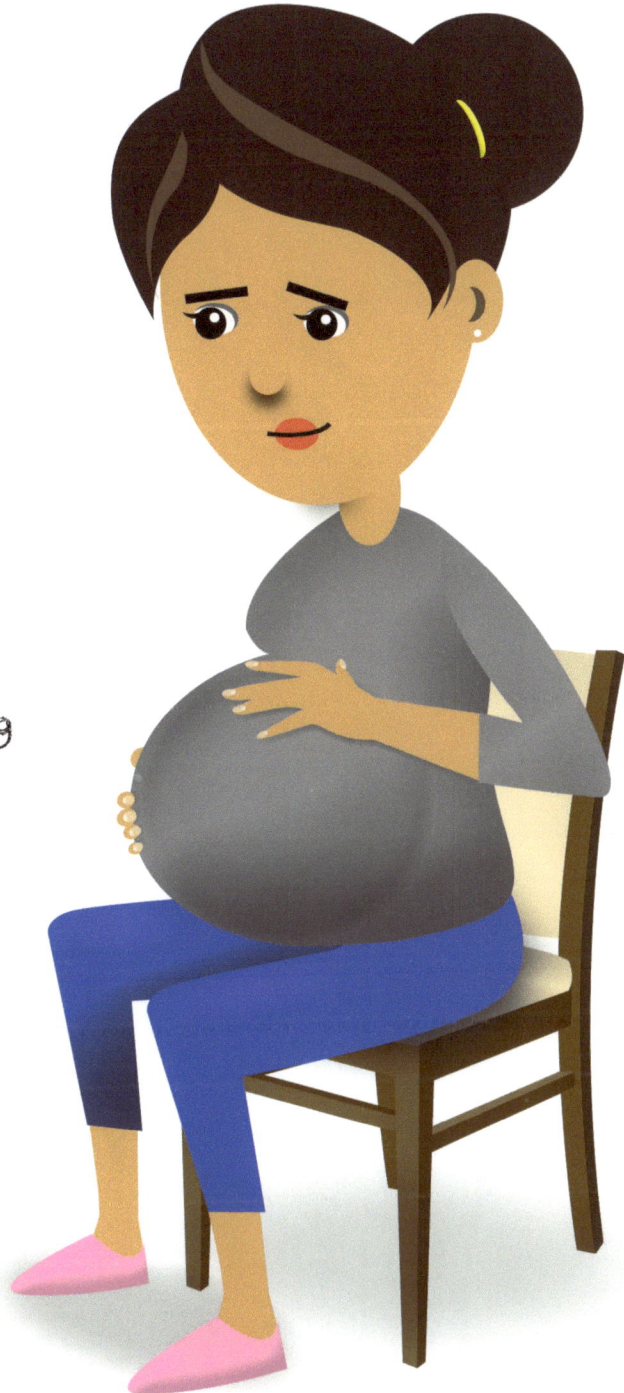

Now that the baby was getting bigger, it would kick in his mom's tummy. Sometimes Kayen could feel the kicks.

Kayen would also sing songs to her tummy because the baby can hear everything.

When it was close to 9 months, Kayen's dad picked him up early from school. As they were driving, his dad pointed to a sign on the road with a big letter H in a blue square. "The H stands for hospital, which is to the right," he said. "Someone special is waiting to meet you there."

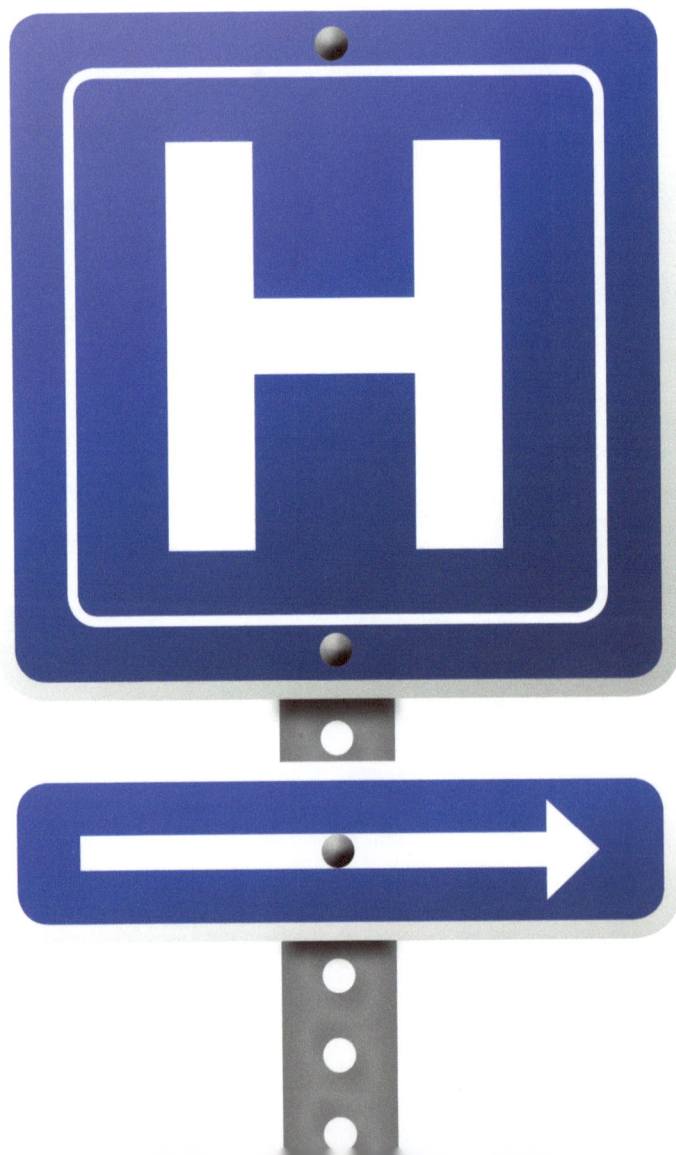

As Kayen's dad turned the car to the right, he saw an even bigger building with bigger windows than the doctor's office. It was the hospital.

1343

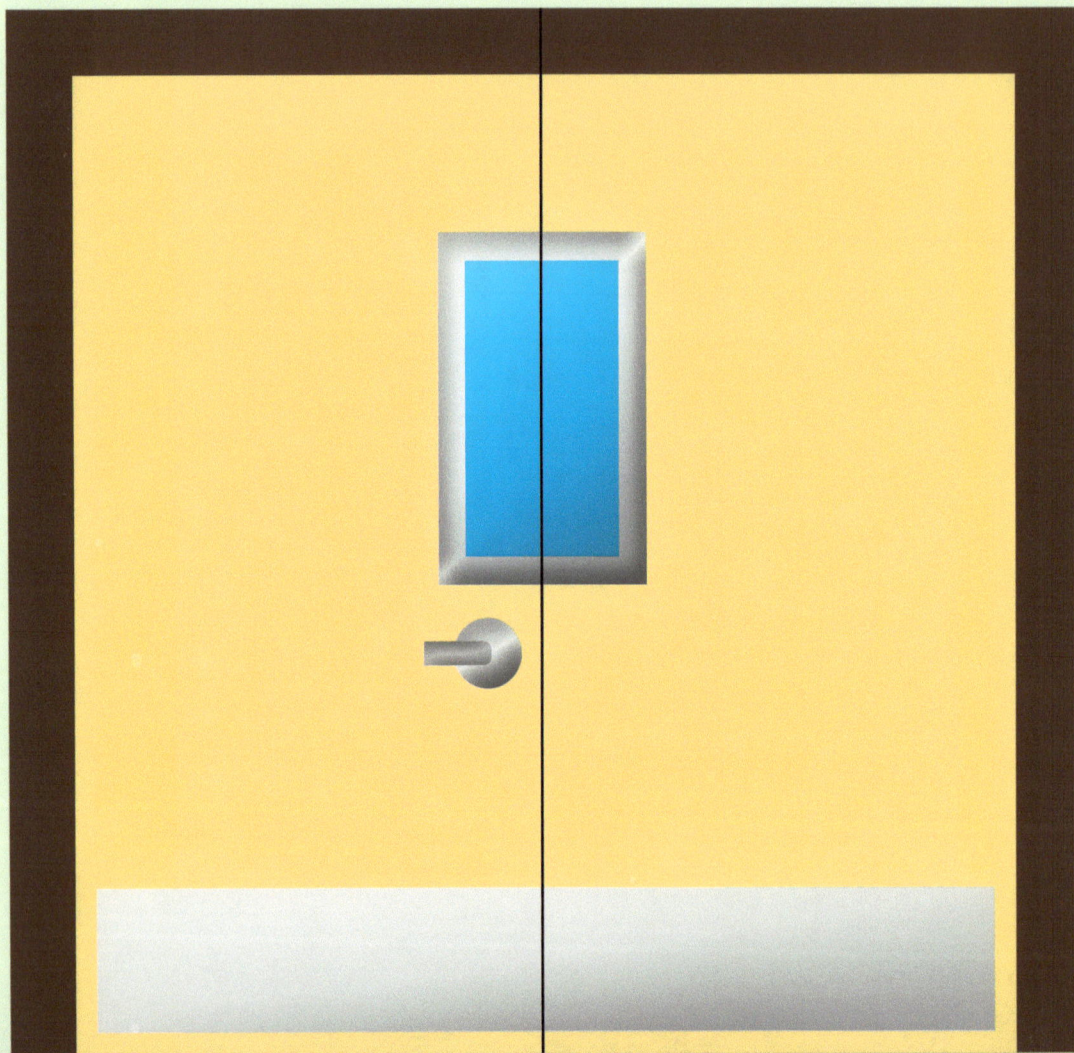

When they walked into the hospital, Kayen's dad took him
to Room 1343.

Kayen walked into room 1343 and saw his mom holding something. It was all bundled up. His dad brought it to him. Who or what could it be???

It was his baby sister and they named her Laiya! Kayen was officially a big brother! He gave his baby sister a big kiss and promised to be the best big brother in the world.

the end!